# The
# GOLFER'S LOG BOOK

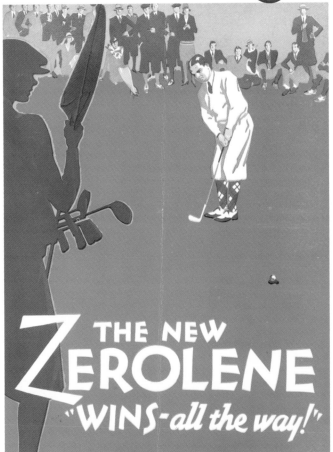

THE NEW
ZEROLENE
"WINS-all the way!"

**A BULFINCH PRESS BOOK**
*Little, Brown and Company • Boston, New York, Toronto, London*

# COPYRIGHTS

Cover:
*Golf.* Lepas.
Collection of Sarah Fabian Baddiel, London.

Title page:
Zerolene. Artist unknown.
Wood River Gallery.

Contents page:
Donald Duck.
Collection of Sarah Fabian Baddiel, London.

# CONTENTS

●

# ROUNDS PLAYED

| | | |
|---|---|---|
| **GOLF COURSE** | Plumavera 54 | DATE 4/16 |
| PAR | 9 17 putts | YARDAGE |

| | | |
|---|---|---|
| SELF | | SCORE | HANDICAP |
| PARTNER 1 | | SCORE | HANDICAP |
| PARTNER 2 | | SCORE | HANDICAP |
| PARTNER 3 | | SCORE | HANDICAP |
| COMMENTS | | |

| | | |
|---|---|---|
| **GOLF COURSE** | | DATE |
| PAR | | YARDAGE |

| | | |
|---|---|---|
| SELF | | SCORE | HANDICAP |
| PARTNER 1 | | SCORE | HANDICAP |
| PARTNER 2 | | SCORE | HANDICAP |
| PARTNER 3 | | SCORE | HANDICAP |
| COMMENTS | | |

*Harper's*. April 1898. Artist unknown.
Wood River Gallery.

5

# ROUNDS PLAYED

**GOLF COURSE** _____ DATE _____

| PAR | YARDAGE |

| SELF | SCORE | HANDICAP |
| PARTNER 1 | SCORE | HANDICAP |
| PARTNER 2 | SCORE | HANDICAP |
| PARTNER 3 | SCORE | HANDICAP |

COMMENTS

---

**GOLF COURSE** _____ DATE _____

| PAR | YARDAGE |

| SELF | SCORE | HANDICAP |
| PARTNER 1 | SCORE | HANDICAP |
| PARTNER 2 | SCORE | HANDICAP |
| PARTNER 3 | SCORE | HANDICAP |

COMMENTS

6

_Outing._ Artist unknown.
Collection of Karen and Ralph Elder.

**Outing**

# HARPER'S WEEKLY

EDITED BY

GEORGE HARVEY

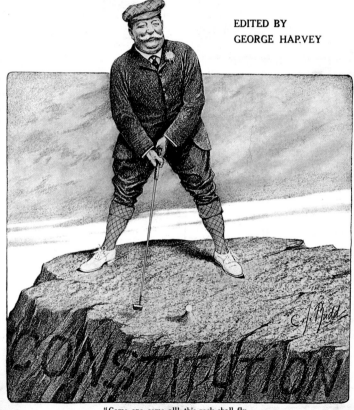

"Come one, come all! this rock shall fly
From its firm base as soon as I."

August 31 1912        HARPER & BROTHERS, N. Y.        Price 10 Cents

# ROUNDS PLAYED

●

**GOLF COURSE** _____ DATE _____

PAR _____ YARDAGE _____

SELF _____ SCORE _____ HANDICAP _____

PARTNER 1 _____ SCORE _____ HANDICAP _____

PARTNER 2 _____ SCORE _____ HANDICAP _____

PARTNER 3 _____ SCORE _____ HANDICAP _____

COMMENTS _____

_____

_____


**GOLF COURSE** _____ DATE _____

PAR _____ YARDAGE _____

SELF _____ SCORE _____ HANDICAP _____

PARTNER 1 _____ SCORE _____ HANDICAP _____

PARTNER 2 _____ SCORE _____ HANDICAP _____

PARTNER 3 _____ SCORE _____ HANDICAP _____

COMMENTS _____

_____

_____

_Harper's Weekly_ [President William Taft].
August 31, 1912.
C. F. Budd. Wood River Gallery.

9

# ROUNDS PLAYED

**GOLF COURSE**

DATE

PAR

YARDAGE

SELF

SCORE          HANDICAP

PARTNER 1

SCORE          HANDICAP

PARTNER 2

SCORE          HANDICAP

PARTNER 3

SCORE          HANDICAP

COMMENTS

**GOLF COURSE**

DATE

PAR

YARDAGE

SELF

SCORE          HANDICAP

PARTNER 1

SCORE          HANDICAP

PARTNER 2

SCORE          HANDICAP

PARTNER 3

SCORE          HANDICAP

COMMENTS

10

Crawford's Assorted Scotch Shortbread.
1928. Artist unknown.
Collection of Karen and Ralph Elder.

By Appointment

"Leading"

# CRAWFORD'S
## ASSORTED
# SCOTCH SHORTBREAD
### THE SHORTBREAD OF TRADITION.
Delightful for Afternoon Tea and Social Functions.

# ROUNDS PLAYED

●

**GOLF COURSE** _____ DATE _____

PAR _____ YARDAGE _____

SELF _____ SCORE _____ HANDICAP _____

PARTNER 1 _____ SCORE _____ HANDICAP _____

PARTNER 2 _____ SCORE _____ HANDICAP _____

PARTNER 3 _____ SCORE _____ HANDICAP _____

COMMENTS _____


**GOLF COURSE** _____ DATE _____

PAR _____ YARDAGE _____

SELF _____ SCORE _____ HANDICAP _____

PARTNER 1 _____ SCORE _____ HANDICAP _____

PARTNER 2 _____ SCORE _____ HANDICAP _____

PARTNER 3 _____ SCORE _____ HANDICAP _____

COMMENTS _____

Artist unknown. Collection of
Sarah Fabian Baddiel, London.

●

# ROUNDS PLAYED

●

**GOLF COURSE** _____ DATE _____

PAR _____ YARDAGE _____

SELF _____ SCORE _____ HANDICAP _____

PARTNER 1 _____ SCORE _____ HANDICAP _____

PARTNER 2 _____ SCORE _____ HANDICAP _____

PARTNER 3 _____ SCORE _____ HANDICAP _____

COMMENTS _____

_____

_____


**GOLF COURSE** _____ DATE _____

PAR _____ YARDAGE _____

SELF _____ SCORE _____ HANDICAP _____

PARTNER 1 _____ SCORE _____ HANDICAP _____

PARTNER 2 _____ SCORE _____ HANDICAP _____

PARTNER 3 _____ SCORE _____ HANDICAP _____

COMMENTS _____

_____

_____

●

*Harper's Round Table Christmas.*
Maxfield Parrish.
Collection of Karen and Ralph Elder.

# HARPER'S
# ROVND TABLE

MAXFIELD PARRISH

# CHRISTMAS

# ROUNDS PLAYED

**GOLF COURSE**

PAR

SELF

PARTNER 1

PARTNER 2

PARTNER 3

COMMENTS

DATE

YARDAGE

SCORE        HANDICAP

SCORE        HANDICAP

SCORE        HANDICAP

SCORE        HANDICAP


**GOLF COURSE**

PAR

SELF

PARTNER 1

PARTNER 2

PARTNER 3

COMMENTS

DATE

YARDAGE

SCORE        HANDICAP

SCORE        HANDICAP

SCORE        HANDICAP

SCORE        HANDICAP


Great Eastern Railway. Circa 1920.
John Hassall. Wood River Gallery.

# ROUNDS PLAYED

●

**GOLF COURSE**

DATE

PAR

YARDAGE

SELF

SCORE          HANDICAP

PARTNER 1

SCORE          HANDICAP

PARTNER 2

SCORE          HANDICAP

PARTNER 3

SCORE          HANDICAP

COMMENTS

**GOLF COURSE**

DATE

PAR

YARDAGE

SELF

SCORE          HANDICAP

PARTNER 1

SCORE          HANDICAP

PARTNER 2

SCORE          HANDICAP

PARTNER 3

SCORE          HANDICAP

COMMENTS

18

●

La Cañada Fruit Growers' Association.
Artist unknown. Wood River Gallery.

BY WILMOT LUNT       THE GOLF GIRL

# ROUNDS PLAYED

●

**GOLF COURSE** _____  DATE _____

PAR _____  YARDAGE _____

SELF _____  SCORE _____  HANDICAP _____

PARTNER 1 _____  SCORE _____  HANDICAP _____

PARTNER 2 _____  SCORE _____  HANDICAP _____

PARTNER 3 _____  SCORE _____  HANDICAP _____

COMMENTS _____

_____

_____


**GOLF COURSE** _____  DATE _____

PAR _____  YARDAGE _____

SELF _____  SCORE _____  HANDICAP _____

PARTNER 1 _____  SCORE _____  HANDICAP _____

PARTNER 2 _____  SCORE _____  HANDICAP _____

PARTNER 3 _____  SCORE _____  HANDICAP _____

COMMENTS _____

_____

_____


_The Golf Girl._ Wilmot Lunt.
Collection of Karen and Ralph Elder.

21

●

# ROUNDS PLAYED

●

**GOLF COURSE** | DATE

PAR | YARDAGE

SELF | SCORE | HANDICAP

PARTNER 1 | SCORE | HANDICAP

PARTNER 2 | SCORE | HANDICAP

PARTNER 3 | SCORE | HANDICAP

COMMENTS

---

**GOLF COURSE** | DATE

PAR | YARDAGE

SELF | SCORE | HANDICAP

PARTNER 1 | SCORE | HANDICAP

PARTNER 2 | SCORE | HANDICAP

PARTNER 3 | SCORE | HANDICAP

COMMENTS

22
●

The Ford Motor Company. 1930.
Artist unknown. Wood River Gallery.

# An admired grace of line and contour

SEEING the new Ford as it speeds along the broad highway or parked proudly beside the cool green of the Country Club, you are impressed by its flowing grace of line and contour. There is about it, in appearance and perform-ance, a substantial excellence which sets it apart and gives it character and position unusual in a low-priced car. To women especially, its safety, its comfort, its reliability and its surprising ease of operation and control have put a new joy in motoring.     «     «     «     «     «     «     «     «

THE NEW FORD COUPE

60e Année. No 38     Le Numéro : 1 fr. 50     Samedi 23 Septembre 1922

# LA VIE PARISIENNE

Imprimerie, Administration et Publicité : 26, rue Tronchet, Paris.

# ROUNDS PLAYED

●

**GOLF COURSE**                                                DATE

PAR                                                            YARDAGE

SELF                                                           SCORE          HANDICAP

PARTNER 1                                                      SCORE          HANDICAP

PARTNER 2                                                      SCORE          HANDICAP

PARTNER 3                                                      SCORE          HANDICAP

COMMENTS


**GOLF COURSE**                                                DATE

PAR                                                            YARDAGE

SELF                                                           SCORE          HANDICAP

PARTNER 1                                                      SCORE          HANDICAP

PARTNER 2                                                      SCORE          HANDICAP

PARTNER 3                                                      SCORE          HANDICAP

COMMENTS


*La Vie Parisienne.* September 23, 1922.
Herouard. Wood River Gallery.

25

●

# ROUNDS PLAYED

●

**GOLF COURSE**

DATE

PAR

YARDAGE

SELF

SCORE          HANDICAP

PARTNER 1

SCORE          HANDICAP

PARTNER 2

SCORE          HANDICAP

PARTNER 3

SCORE          HANDICAP

COMMENTS

**GOLF COURSE**

DATE

PAR

YARDAGE

SELF

SCORE          HANDICAP

PARTNER 1

SCORE          HANDICAP

PARTNER 2

SCORE          HANDICAP

PARTNER 3

SCORE          HANDICAP

COMMENTS

Interwoven Toe and Heel Socks.
Norman Rockwell.
Collection of Karen and Ralph Elder.

# BOBBY JONES *on*

# GOLF

BOBBY JONES
REVEALS THE
NEWEST SECRETS OF
HIS GOLFING SUCCESS

REVISED
EDITION

Introduction by
GRANTLAND RICE

GOLF RULES

GOLF CONCENTRATION

PUTTING PSYCHOLOGY

THE SOUND GOLF SWING

IMPORTANCE OF BACKSWING

ILLUMINATING ARTICLES ON
PUTTING—STANCE—SWING—
GRIP—CORRECTING FAULTS—
WITH TWENTY-FIVE OTHER
INSTRUCTIVE ARTICLES

# ROUNDS PLAYED

●

**GOLF COURSE** _____  DATE _____

PAR _____  YARDAGE _____

SELF _____  SCORE _____  HANDICAP _____

PARTNER 1 _____  SCORE _____  HANDICAP _____

PARTNER 2 _____  SCORE _____  HANDICAP _____

PARTNER 3 _____  SCORE _____  HANDICAP _____

COMMENTS _____

_____

_____


**GOLF COURSE** _____  DATE _____

PAR _____  YARDAGE _____

SELF _____  SCORE _____  HANDICAP _____

PARTNER 1 _____  SCORE _____  HANDICAP _____

PARTNER 2 _____  SCORE _____  HANDICAP _____

PARTNER 3 _____  SCORE _____  HANDICAP _____

COMMENTS _____

_____

_____

*Bobby Jones on Golf,* revised edition.
Artist unknown. Collection of
Sarah Fabian Baddiel, London.

●

# ROUNDS PLAYED

**GOLF COURSE**

DATE

PAR

YARDAGE

SELF

SCORE

HANDICAP

PARTNER 1

SCORE

HANDICAP

PARTNER 2

SCORE

HANDICAP

PARTNER 3

SCORE

HANDICAP

COMMENTS

**GOLF COURSE**

DATE

PAR

YARDAGE

SELF

SCORE

HANDICAP

PARTNER 1

SCORE

HANDICAP

PARTNER 2

SCORE

HANDICAP

PARTNER 3

SCORE

HANDICAP

COMMENTS

*The Golf Girl.* Circa 1900. Rob Wagner.
Courtesy of Kennedy Galleries, Inc.,
New York. Photo courtesy of Sally Fox,
The Picture Company.

# THE GOLF GIRL

# ROUNDS PLAYED

●

**GOLF COURSE** _____ DATE _____

PAR _____ YARDAGE _____

SELF _____ SCORE _____ HANDICAP _____

PARTNER 1 _____ SCORE _____ HANDICAP _____

PARTNER 2 _____ SCORE _____ HANDICAP _____

PARTNER 3 _____ SCORE _____ HANDICAP _____

COMMENTS _____

_____

_____


**GOLF COURSE** _____ DATE _____

PAR _____ YARDAGE _____

SELF _____ SCORE _____ HANDICAP _____

PARTNER 1 _____ SCORE _____ HANDICAP _____

PARTNER 2 _____ SCORE _____ HANDICAP _____

PARTNER 3 _____ SCORE _____ HANDICAP _____

COMMENTS _____

_____

_____

*Golf.* A. Meiresonne. Collection of
Sarah Fabian Baddiel, London.

33

●

# ROUNDS PLAYED

**GOLF COURSE**

DATE

PAR

YARDAGE

SELF

SCORE

HANDICAP

PARTNER 1

SCORE

HANDICAP

PARTNER 2

SCORE

HANDICAP

PARTNER 3

SCORE

HANDICAP

COMMENTS

---

**GOLF COURSE**

DATE

PAR

YARDAGE

SELF

SCORE

HANDICAP

PARTNER 1

SCORE

HANDICAP

PARTNER 2

SCORE

HANDICAP

PARTNER 3

SCORE

HANDICAP

COMMENTS

34

Artist unknown. Collection of Sarah
Fabian Baddiel, London.

# ROUNDS PLAYED

●

| GOLF COURSE | DATE | |
|---|---|---|
| PAR | YARDAGE | |
| SELF | SCORE | HANDICAP |
| PARTNER 1 | SCORE | HANDICAP |
| PARTNER 2 | SCORE | HANDICAP |
| PARTNER 3 | SCORE | HANDICAP |
| COMMENTS | | |

| GOLF COURSE | DATE | |
|---|---|---|
| PAR | YARDAGE | |
| SELF | SCORE | HANDICAP |
| PARTNER 1 | SCORE | HANDICAP |
| PARTNER 2 | SCORE | HANDICAP |
| PARTNER 3 | SCORE | HANDICAP |
| COMMENTS | | |

●

# ROUNDS PLAYED

●

**GOLF COURSE**

DATE

PAR | YARDAGE

SELF | SCORE | HANDICAP

PARTNER 1 | SCORE | HANDICAP

PARTNER 2 | SCORE | HANDICAP

PARTNER 3 | SCORE | HANDICAP

COMMENTS

**GOLF COURSE**

DATE

PAR | YARDAGE

SELF | SCORE | HANDICAP

PARTNER 1 | SCORE | HANDICAP

PARTNER 2 | SCORE | HANDICAP

PARTNER 3 | SCORE | HANDICAP

COMMENTS

38

●

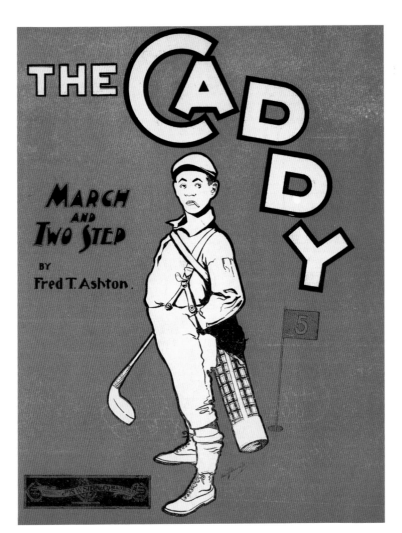

# ROUNDS PLAYED

●

**GOLF COURSE** _____

DATE _____

PAR _____

YARDAGE _____

SELF _____

SCORE _____ HANDICAP _____

PARTNER 1 _____

SCORE _____ HANDICAP _____

PARTNER 2 _____

SCORE _____ HANDICAP _____

PARTNER 3 _____

SCORE _____ HANDICAP _____

COMMENTS _____

_____

_____


**GOLF COURSE** _____

DATE _____

PAR _____

YARDAGE _____

SELF _____

SCORE _____ HANDICAP _____

PARTNER 1 _____

SCORE _____ HANDICAP _____

PARTNER 2 _____

SCORE _____ HANDICAP _____

PARTNER 3 _____

SCORE _____ HANDICAP _____

COMMENTS _____

_____

_____

*Collier's*. August 18, 1934.
Arthur Crouch. Wood River Gallery.

41

●

# ROUNDS PLAYED

●

**GOLF COURSE**

DATE

PAR

YARDAGE

SELF

SCORE          HANDICAP

PARTNER 1

SCORE          HANDICAP

PARTNER 2

SCORE          HANDICAP

PARTNER 3

SCORE          HANDICAP

COMMENTS

**GOLF COURSE**

DATE

PAR

YARDAGE

SELF

SCORE          HANDICAP

PARTNER 1

SCORE          HANDICAP

PARTNER 2

SCORE          HANDICAP

PARTNER 3

SCORE          HANDICAP

COMMENTS

●

Bradley Knitting Company.
Artist unknown. Wood River Gallery.

OPINIONS may vary as to whether the gentleman's *stance* is correct. But one thing is certain. He is *dressed* exactly right. For he is wearing one of the new Bradley golf combinations—a knitted pullover sweater and stockings to match.

One is certain to find himself frequently in the presence of these unusually effective, matched outfits this season. Quite as often, perhaps, as ¡though he played the fashionable courses at Gleneagles or St. Andrews.

Your Bradley dealer is now showing the

smart Bradley golf combinations with matching stockings. He offers them with pull-over, straight buttoned jackets or buttoned blouses. The colors range from the most inconspicuous shades to the gayest of Glasgow plaids. Try them on. See what a difference they make.

Note particularly the trim, comfortable fit, the sturdy elastic knitting, the reasonable prices—$12 to $20 per set. These are advantages always found in every Bradley-knit garment. Above all else, look for the Bradley label. For 20 years this famous label has been an unfailing index to satisfaction and genuine economy in all types of knitted outerwear.

\* \* \*

Copies of Bradley's booklets "Spring and Summer Styles" and "How to Swim" will be sent to any address, postpaid, upon request.

BRADLEY     KNITTING     COMPANY,     DELAVAN,     WIS.

*Golf*
*Number*

# Life

Price 15 Cents

October 14, 1920

Vol. 76.   Copyright, 1920, Life Publishing Company   No. 1980

*"Fore!"*

# ROUNDS PLAYED

•

**GOLF COURSE**

DATE

PAR

YARDAGE

SELF

SCORE          HANDICAP

PARTNER 1

SCORE          HANDICAP

PARTNER 2

SCORE          HANDICAP

PARTNER 3

SCORE          HANDICAP

COMMENTS

---

**GOLF COURSE**

DATE

PAR

YARDAGE

SELF

SCORE          HANDICAP

PARTNER 1

SCORE          HANDICAP

PARTNER 2

SCORE          HANDICAP

PARTNER 3

SCORE          HANDICAP

COMMENTS

---

*Life*. October 14, 1920. Coles Phillips.
Wood River Gallery.

•

# ROUNDS PLAYED

**GOLF COURSE**

DATE

PAR

YARDAGE

SELF

SCORE          HANDICAP

PARTNER 1

SCORE          HANDICAP

PARTNER 2

SCORE          HANDICAP

PARTNER 3

SCORE          HANDICAP

COMMENTS

**GOLF COURSE**

DATE

PAR

YARDAGE

SELF

SCORE          HANDICAP

PARTNER 1

SCORE          HANDICAP

PARTNER 2

SCORE          HANDICAP

PARTNER 3

SCORE          HANDICAP

COMMENTS

*Life*. May 8, 1931. Ed Graham.
Collection of Karen and Ralph Elder.

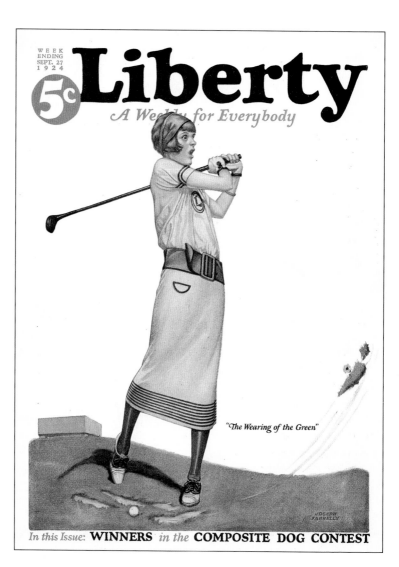

WEEK
ENDING
SEPT. 27
1924

5¢

# Liberty

*A Weekly for Everybody*

"The Wearing of the Green"

JOSEPH
FARRELLY

In this Issue: **WINNERS** *in the* **COMPOSITE DOG CONTEST**

# ROUNDS PLAYED

●

**GOLF COURSE** _____ DATE _____

PAR _____ YARDAGE _____

SELF _____ SCORE _____ HANDICAP _____

PARTNER 1 _____ SCORE _____ HANDICAP _____

PARTNER 2 _____ SCORE _____ HANDICAP _____

PARTNER 3 _____ SCORE _____ HANDICAP _____

COMMENTS _____

_____

_____

**GOLF COURSE** _____ DATE _____

PAR _____ YARDAGE _____

SELF _____ SCORE _____ HANDICAP _____

PARTNER 1 _____ SCORE _____ HANDICAP _____

PARTNER 2 _____ SCORE _____ HANDICAP _____

PARTNER 3 _____ SCORE _____ HANDICAP _____

COMMENTS _____

_____

_____

*Liberty.* September 27, 1924.
Joseph Farrelly.
Collection of Karen and Ralph Elder.

●

# ROUNDS PLAYED

**GOLF COURSE**

DATE

PAR

YARDAGE

SELF

SCORE   HANDICAP

PARTNER 1

SCORE   HANDICAP

PARTNER 2

SCORE   HANDICAP

PARTNER 3

SCORE   HANDICAP

COMMENTS

**GOLF COURSE**

DATE

PAR

YARDAGE

SELF

SCORE   HANDICAP

PARTNER 1

SCORE   HANDICAP

PARTNER 2

SCORE   HANDICAP

PARTNER 3

SCORE   HANDICAP

COMMENTS

Dunlop Figurine. Artist unknown.
Collection of Sarah Fabian Baddiel,
London.

WE play DUNLOP

# ROUNDS PLAYED

●

| GOLF COURSE | DATE | |
|---|---|---|
| PAR | YARDAGE | |
| SELF | SCORE | HANDICAP |
| PARTNER 1 | SCORE | HANDICAP |
| PARTNER 2 | SCORE | HANDICAP |
| PARTNER 3 | SCORE | HANDICAP |
| COMMENTS | | |

| GOLF COURSE | DATE | |
|---|---|---|
| PAR | YARDAGE | |
| SELF | SCORE | HANDICAP |
| PARTNER 1 | SCORE | HANDICAP |
| PARTNER 2 | SCORE | HANDICAP |
| PARTNER 3 | SCORE | HANDICAP |
| COMMENTS | | |

*Blanco y Negro.* Artist unknown.
Collection of Sarah Fabian Baddiel,
London.

●

# ROUNDS PLAYED

**GOLF COURSE**

DATE

PAR

YARDAGE

SELF

SCORE          HANDICAP

PARTNER 1

SCORE          HANDICAP

PARTNER 2

SCORE          HANDICAP

PARTNER 3

SCORE          HANDICAP

COMMENTS

**GOLF COURSE**

DATE

PAR

YARDAGE

SELF

SCORE          HANDICAP

PARTNER 1

SCORE          HANDICAP

PARTNER 2

SCORE          HANDICAP

PARTNER 3

SCORE          HANDICAP

COMMENTS

*Le Sourire.* Aquarelle de Jaquelux.
Collection of Sarah Fabian Baddiel,
London.

28ᵉ Année, Nᵒ 410     Prix : 1 Fr. 50     JEUDI 12 MARS 1925

**GOLF**
Il n'arrive jamais à mettre dans le trou.

*Aquarelle de Jaquelux*

# INN DIXIE

JUNE, 1935

VOL. 2   NO. 6

**A MONTHLY MAGAZINE FOR GUESTS OF DINKLER HOTELS**

# ROUNDS PLAYED

●

**GOLF COURSE** _____  DATE _____

PAR _____  YARDAGE _____

SELF _____  SCORE _____  HANDICAP _____

PARTNER 1 _____  SCORE _____  HANDICAP _____

PARTNER 2 _____  SCORE _____  HANDICAP _____

PARTNER 3 _____  SCORE _____  HANDICAP _____

COMMENTS _____



**GOLF COURSE** _____  DATE _____

PAR _____  YARDAGE _____

SELF _____  SCORE _____  HANDICAP _____

PARTNER 1 _____  SCORE _____  HANDICAP _____

PARTNER 2 _____  SCORE _____  HANDICAP _____

PARTNER 3 _____  SCORE _____  HANDICAP _____

COMMENTS _____

_Inn Dixie._ June 1935. Artist unknown.
Wood River Gallery.

57

●

# ROUNDS PLAYED

**GOLF COURSE**

DATE

PAR

YARDAGE

SELF

SCORE ___ HANDICAP ___

PARTNER 1

SCORE ___ HANDICAP ___

PARTNER 2

SCORE ___ HANDICAP ___

PARTNER 3

SCORE ___ HANDICAP ___

COMMENTS

---

**GOLF COURSE**

DATE

PAR

YARDAGE

SELF

SCORE ___ HANDICAP ___

PARTNER 1

SCORE ___ HANDICAP ___

PARTNER 2

SCORE ___ HANDICAP ___

PARTNER 3

SCORE ___ HANDICAP ___

COMMENTS

Sports d'Été et d'Hiver
Station d'altitude 1550 m.(5000 Feet)
MONTANA-VERMALA
S/SIERRE (SUISSE)

# ROUNDS PLAYED

●

**GOLF COURSE**

DATE

PAR

YARDAGE

SELF

SCORE          HANDICAP

PARTNER 1

SCORE          HANDICAP

PARTNER 2

SCORE          HANDICAP

PARTNER 3

SCORE          HANDICAP

COMMENTS

---

**GOLF COURSE**

DATE

PAR

YARDAGE

SELF

SCORE          HANDICAP

PARTNER 1

SCORE          HANDICAP

PARTNER 2

SCORE          HANDICAP

PARTNER 3

SCORE          HANDICAP

COMMENTS

Montana-Vermala travel poster.
Circa 1930. Artist unknown.
Wood River Gallery.

# ROUNDS PLAYED

**GOLF COURSE**

DATE

PAR

YARDAGE

SELF

SCORE                HANDICAP

PARTNER 1

SCORE                HANDICAP

PARTNER 2

SCORE                HANDICAP

PARTNER 3

SCORE                HANDICAP

COMMENTS


**GOLF COURSE**

DATE

PAR

YARDAGE

SELF

SCORE                HANDICAP

PARTNER 1

SCORE                HANDICAP

PARTNER 2

SCORE                HANDICAP

PARTNER 3

SCORE                HANDICAP

COMMENTS

Vichy Ses Sources travel poster.
Circa 1920. Artist unknown.
Wood River Gallery.

golf de Sarlabot
houlgate – cabourg

# ROUNDS PLAYED

GOLF COURSE _____ DATE _____

PAR _____ YARDAGE _____

SELF _____ SCORE _____ HANDICAP _____

PARTNER 1 _____ SCORE _____ HANDICAP _____

PARTNER 2 _____ SCORE _____ HANDICAP _____

PARTNER 3 _____ SCORE _____ HANDICAP _____

COMMENTS _____


GOLF COURSE _____ DATE _____

PAR _____ YARDAGE _____

SELF _____ SCORE _____ HANDICAP _____

PARTNER 1 _____ SCORE _____ HANDICAP _____

PARTNER 2 _____ SCORE _____ HANDICAP _____

PARTNER 3 _____ SCORE _____ HANDICAP _____

COMMENTS _____

# ROUNDS PLAYED

**GOLF COURSE**

DATE

PAR

YARDAGE

SELF

SCORE

HANDICAP

PARTNER 1

SCORE

HANDICAP

PARTNER 2

SCORE

HANDICAP

PARTNER 3

SCORE

HANDICAP

COMMENTS

**GOLF COURSE**

DATE

PAR

YARDAGE

SELF

SCORE

HANDICAP

PARTNER 1

SCORE

HANDICAP

PARTNER 2

SCORE

HANDICAP

PARTNER 3

SCORE

HANDICAP

COMMENTS

*Biarritz Illustré.* 1927. J. C. Haramboure. Laget Collection. Photo courtesy of Sally Fox, The Picture Company.

N° 6 (Nouvelle Série)　　　　Le Numéro : 2 fr. 50　　　　30 Septembre 1927

# Biarritz Illustré
## et Côte Basque Pyrénées

cette revue officielle est en lecture dans 1000 hotels, casinos, cercles, syndicats de la région, pyrénées côte basque, gascogne et dans le monde entier

J.C. Haramboure

LIST OF VISITORS　　　　　　　　LISTA DE EXTRANJEROS

## Liste
## Officielle des Étrangers

publiée sous le haut patronage de la Fédération des Syndicats d'Initiative des Pyrénées côte Basque et Gascogne

# ROUNDS PLAYED

●

**GOLF COURSE**

PAR

SELF

PARTNER 1

PARTNER 2

PARTNER 3

COMMENTS

DATE

YARDAGE

SCORE          HANDICAP

SCORE          HANDICAP

SCORE          HANDICAP

SCORE          HANDICAP

---

**GOLF COURSE**

PAR

SELF

PARTNER 1

PARTNER 2

PARTNER 3

COMMENTS

DATE

YARDAGE

SCORE          HANDICAP

SCORE          HANDICAP

SCORE          HANDICAP

SCORE          HANDICAP

Le Touquet travel poster.
Circa 1930. Artist unknown.
Wood River Gallery.

●

# ROUNDS PLAYED

**GOLF COURSE**

DATE

PAR

YARDAGE

SELF

SCORE                HANDICAP

PARTNER 1

SCORE                HANDICAP

PARTNER 2

SCORE                HANDICAP

PARTNER 3

SCORE                HANDICAP

COMMENTS

---

**GOLF COURSE**

DATE

PAR

YARDAGE

SELF

SCORE                HANDICAP

PARTNER 1

SCORE                HANDICAP

PARTNER 2

SCORE                HANDICAP

PARTNER 3

SCORE                HANDICAP

COMMENTS

70

Cannes travel poster. Artist unknown.
Wood River Gallery.

CANNES

La Ville des sports élégants

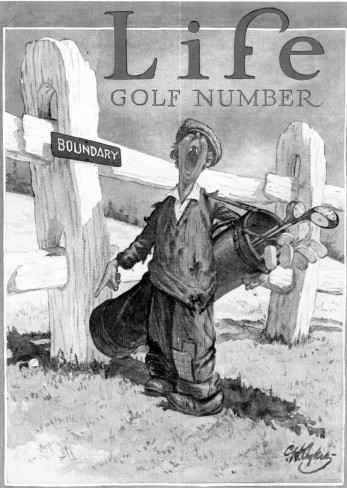

# Life

## GOLF NUMBER

BOUNDARY

May 27 1926

THE KILLJOY

Price 15 cents

# ROUNDS PLAYED

●

**GOLF COURSE**
DATE

PAR
YARDAGE

SELF
SCORE          HANDICAP

PARTNER 1
SCORE          HANDICAP

PARTNER 2
SCORE          HANDICAP

PARTNER 3
SCORE          HANDICAP

COMMENTS

**GOLF COURSE**
DATE

PAR
YARDAGE

SELF
SCORE          HANDICAP

PARTNER 1
SCORE          HANDICAP

PARTNER 2
SCORE          HANDICAP

PARTNER 3
SCORE          HANDICAP

COMMENTS

*Life.* May 27, 1926.
Collection of Karen and Ralph Elder.

●

# ROUNDS PLAYED

**GOLF COURSE**

DATE

PAR

YARDAGE

SELF

SCORE                HANDICAP

PARTNER 1

SCORE                HANDICAP

PARTNER 2

SCORE                HANDICAP

PARTNER 3

SCORE                HANDICAP

COMMENTS

---

**GOLF COURSE**

DATE

PAR

YARDAGE

SELF

SCORE                HANDICAP

PARTNER 1

SCORE                HANDICAP

PARTNER 2

SCORE                HANDICAP

PARTNER 3

SCORE                HANDICAP

COMMENTS

74

*Liberty.* September 28, 1940.
David Berger. Wood River Gallery.

SEPT. 28, 1940

# Liberty

**5¢**

# HOW JAPAN PLANS TO CONQUER AMERICA by Carl Crow
## MURDER ON THE DIAMOND by Joe Medwick

"What should I take here, Caddie?"
"I should take a Guinness, Sir!"

# ROUNDS PLAYED

---

**GOLF COURSE**                                          DATE

PAR                                                      YARDAGE

SELF                                                     SCORE          HANDICAP

PARTNER 1                                                SCORE          HANDICAP

PARTNER 2                                                SCORE          HANDICAP

PARTNER 3                                                SCORE          HANDICAP

COMMENTS

---

**GOLF COURSE**                                          DATE

PAR                                                      YARDAGE

SELF                                                     SCORE          HANDICAP

PARTNER 1                                                SCORE          HANDICAP

PARTNER 2                                                SCORE          HANDICAP

PARTNER 3                                                SCORE          HANDICAP

COMMENTS

---

John Bateman. Collection of Sarah
Fabian Baddiel, London.

77

# ROUNDS PLAYED

●

**GOLF COURSE**

DATE

PAR

YARDAGE

SELF

SCORE          HANDICAP

PARTNER 1

SCORE          HANDICAP

PARTNER 2

SCORE          HANDICAP

PARTNER 3

SCORE          HANDICAP

COMMENTS

---

**GOLF COURSE**

DATE

PAR

YARDAGE

SELF

SCORE          HANDICAP

PARTNER 1

SCORE          HANDICAP

PARTNER 2

SCORE          HANDICAP

PARTNER 3

SCORE          HANDICAP

COMMENTS

●

*Life.* April 21, 1927. L. J. Holton.
Collection of Karen and Ralph Elder.

April 21 1927

Price 15 cents

# Life

## · SPORTS NUMBER ·

L.J.Holton

The Sport of Missing Men

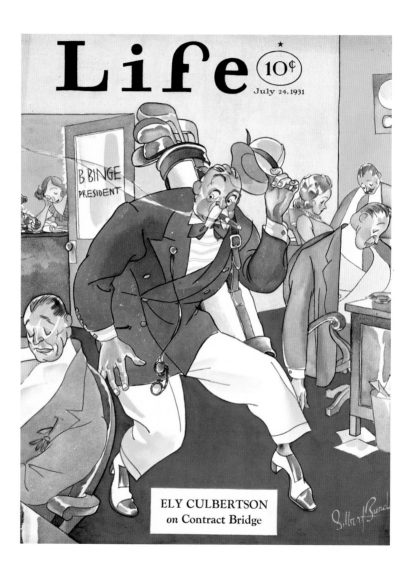

# Life

10¢

July 24, 1931

B. BINGE
PRESIDENT

ELY CULBERTSON
*on* Contract Bridge

# ROUNDS PLAYED

●

**GOLF COURSE** _____ DATE _____

PAR _____ YARDAGE _____

SELF _____ SCORE _____ HANDICAP _____

PARTNER 1 _____ SCORE _____ HANDICAP _____

PARTNER 2 _____ SCORE _____ HANDICAP _____

PARTNER 3 _____ SCORE _____ HANDICAP _____

COMMENTS _____

_____

_____

**GOLF COURSE** _____ DATE _____

PAR _____ YARDAGE _____

SELF _____ SCORE _____ HANDICAP _____

PARTNER 1 _____ SCORE _____ HANDICAP _____

PARTNER 2 _____ SCORE _____ HANDICAP _____

PARTNER 3 _____ SCORE _____ HANDICAP _____

COMMENTS _____

_____

_____

*Life.* July 24, 1931. Gilbert Bunch.
Collection of Karen and Ralph Elder.

●

# ROUNDS PLAYED

**GOLF COURSE**

DATE

PAR

YARDAGE

SELF

SCORE    HANDICAP

PARTNER 1

SCORE    HANDICAP

PARTNER 2

SCORE    HANDICAP

PARTNER 3

SCORE    HANDICAP

COMMENTS

**GOLF COURSE**

DATE

PAR

YARDAGE

SELF

SCORE    HANDICAP

PARTNER 1

SCORE    HANDICAP

PARTNER 2

SCORE    HANDICAP

PARTNER 3

SCORE    HANDICAP

COMMENTS

SOUTHERN
CALIFORNIA

UNION PACIFIC

# GOLF COURSES

## GOLF COURSE

ADDRESS

TEL

PAR

GREEN FEES

YARDAGE

COURSE DESIGNED BY

GOLF PRO

BOOKING RULES

COMMENTS

## GOLF COURSE

ADDRESS

TEL

PAR

GREEN FEES

YARDAGE

COURSE DESIGNED BY

GOLF PRO

BOOKING RULES

COMMENTS

Southern California Union Pacific.
Artist unknown. Wood River Gallery.

# GOLF COURSES

## GOLF COURSE

ADDRESS

TEL

PAR

GREEN FEES

YARDAGE

COURSE DESIGNED BY

GOLF PRO

BOOKING RULES

COMMENTS

## GOLF COURSE

ADDRESS

TEL

PAR

GREEN FEES

YARDAGE

COURSE DESIGNED BY

GOLF PRO

BOOKING RULES

COMMENTS

86

# GOLF COURSES

## GOLF COURSE

ADDRESS

TEL                                    PAR

GREEN FEES                             YARDAGE

COURSE DESIGNED BY

GOLF PRO

BOOKING RULES

COMMENTS

## GOLF COURSE

ADDRESS

TEL                                    PAR

GREEN FEES                             YARDAGE

COURSE DESIGNED BY

GOLF PRO

BOOKING RULES

COMMENTS

# GOLF COURSES

**GOLF COURSE**

ADDRESS

TEL

PAR

GREEN FEES

YARDAGE

COURSE DESIGNED BY

GOLF PRO

BOOKING RULES

COMMENTS

**GOLF COURSE**

ADDRESS

TEL

PAR

GREEN FEES

YARDAGE

COURSE DESIGNED BY

GOLF PRO

BOOKING RULES

COMMENTS

# GOLF COURSES

**GOLF COURSE**

ADDRESS

TEL

GREEN FEES

PAR

YARDAGE

COURSE DESIGNED BY

GOLF PRO

BOOKING RULES

COMMENTS

**GOLF COURSE**

ADDRESS

TEL

GREEN FEES

PAR

YARDAGE

COURSE DESIGNED BY

GOLF PRO

BOOKING RULES

COMMENTS

# GOLF COURSES

**GOLF COURSE**

ADDRESS

TEL

PAR

GREEN FEES

YARDAGE

COURSE DESIGNED BY

GOLF PRO

BOOKING RULES

COMMENTS

**GOLF COURSE**

ADDRESS

TEL

PAR

GREEN FEES

YARDAGE

COURSE DESIGNED BY

GOLF PRO

BOOKING RULES

COMMENTS

# GOLF COURSES

**GOLF COURSE**

ADDRESS

TEL

PAR

GREEN FEES

YARDAGE

COURSE DESIGNED BY

GOLF PRO

BOOKING RULES

COMMENTS

**GOLF COURSE**

ADDRESS

TEL

PAR

GREEN FEES

YARDAGE

COURSE DESIGNED BY

GOLF PRO

BOOKING RULES

COMMENTS

# GOLF COURSES

**GOLF COURSE**

ADDRESS

TEL

PAR

GREEN FEES

YARDAGE

COURSE DESIGNED BY

GOLF PRO

BOOKING RULES

COMMENTS

**GOLF COURSE**

ADDRESS

TEL

PAR

GREEN FEES

YARDAGE

COURSE DESIGNED BY

GOLF PRO

BOOKING RULES

COMMENTS

# GOLF COURSES

●

**GOLF COURSE**

ADDRESS

TEL

PAR

GREEN FEES

YARDAGE

COURSE DESIGNED BY

GOLF PRO

BOOKING RULES

COMMENTS

**GOLF COURSE**

ADDRESS

TEL

PAR

GREEN FEES

YARDAGE

COURSE DESIGNED BY

GOLF PRO

BOOKING RULES

COMMENTS

# GOLF PARTNERS

●

**NAME**

ADDRESS

HANDICAP

COMMENTS

TEL (H)                    TEL (W)                    FAX

**NAME**

ADDRESS

HANDICAP

COMMENTS

TEL (H)                    TEL (W)                    FAX

**NAME**

ADDRESS

HANDICAP

COMMENTS

TEL (H)                    TEL (W)                    FAX

*Life.* 1927. Artist unknown.
Wood River Gallery.

95

●

# GOLF PARTNERS

**NAME**

| ADDRESS | | |
|---|---|---|
| | | |
| HANDICAP | | |
| COMMENTS | | |
| TEL (H) | TEL (W) | FAX |

**NAME**

| ADDRESS | | |
|---|---|---|
| | | |
| HANDICAP | | |
| COMMENTS | | |
| TEL (H) | TEL (W) | FAX |

**NAME**

| ADDRESS | | |
|---|---|---|
| | | |
| HANDICAP | | |
| COMMENTS | | |
| TEL (H) | TEL (W) | FAX |

# GOLF PARTNERS

**NAME**

ADDRESS

HANDICAP

COMMENTS

TEL (H)                            TEL (W)                        FAX

**NAME**

ADDRESS

HANDICAP

COMMENTS

TEL (H)                            TEL (W)                        FAX

**NAME**

ADDRESS

HANDICAP

COMMENTS

TEL (H)                            TEL (W)                        FAX

# GOLF PARTNERS

**NAME**

ADDRESS

HANDICAP

COMMENTS

TEL (H)                    TEL (W)                    FAX

**NAME**

ADDRESS

HANDICAP

COMMENTS

TEL (H)                    TEL (W)                    FAX

**NAME**

ADDRESS

HANDICAP

COMMENTS

TEL (H)                    TEL (W)                    FAX

# GOLF PARTNERS

•

**NAME**

ADDRESS

HANDICAP

COMMENTS

TEL (H)                    TEL (W)                    FAX


**NAME**

ADDRESS

HANDICAP

COMMENTS

TEL (H)                    TEL (W)                    FAX


**NAME**

ADDRESS

HANDICAP

COMMENTS

TEL (H)                    TEL (W)                    FAX

# GOLF PARTNERS

**NAME**

ADDRESS

HANDICAP

COMMENTS

TEL (H)                    TEL (W)                    FAX

**NAME**

ADDRESS

HANDICAP

COMMENTS

TEL (H)                    TEL (W)                    FAX

**NAME**

ADDRESS

HANDICAP

COMMENTS

TEL (H)                    TEL (W)                    FAX

# GOLF PARTNERS

**NAME**

ADDRESS

HANDICAP

COMMENTS

TEL (H)        TEL (W)        FAX

**NAME**

ADDRESS

HANDICAP

COMMENTS

TEL (H)        TEL (W)        FAX

**NAME**

ADDRESS

HANDICAP

COMMENTS

TEL (H)        TEL (W)        FAX

# GOLF PARTNERS

NAME

ADDRESS

HANDICAP

COMMENTS

TEL (H)                    TEL (W)                    FAX


NAME

ADDRESS

HANDICAP

COMMENTS

TEL (H)                    TEL (W)                    FAX


NAME

ADDRESS

HANDICAP

COMMENTS

TEL (H)                    TEL (W)                    FAX

103

# GOLF PARTNERS

**NAME**

ADDRESS

HANDICAP

COMMENTS

TEL (H)                    TEL (W)                    FAX

**NAME**

ADDRESS

HANDICAP

COMMENTS

TEL (H)                    TEL (W)                    FAX

**NAME**

ADDRESS

HANDICAP

COMMENTS

TEL (H)                    TEL (W)                    FAX

# GOLF PARTNERS

**NAME**

ADDRESS

HANDICAP

COMMENTS

TEL (H)                    TEL (W)                    FAX


**NAME**

ADDRESS

HANDICAP

COMMENTS

TEL (H)                    TEL (W)                    FAX


**NAME**

ADDRESS

HANDICAP

COMMENTS

TEL (H)                    TEL (W)                    FAX

# GOLF PARTNERS

●

**NAME**

ADDRESS

HANDICAP

COMMENTS

TEL (H)          TEL (W)          FAX

**NAME**

ADDRESS

HANDICAP

COMMENTS

TEL (H)          TEL (W)          FAX

**NAME**

ADDRESS

HANDICAP

COMMENTS

TEL (H)          TEL (W)          FAX

# GOLF PARTNERS

**NAME**

ADDRESS

HANDICAP

COMMENTS

TEL (H)                          TEL (W)                          FAX

**NAME**

ADDRESS

HANDICAP

COMMENTS

TEL (H)                          TEL (W)                          FAX

**NAME**

ADDRESS

HANDICAP

COMMENTS

TEL (H)                          TEL (W)                          FAX

# GOLF GAMES

There are many different ways to play golf — *play* in the sense of scoring and competing person against person, or team against team. In this section there are games that are designed for every conceivable level of player.

**STROKE PLAY**   The simplest and most common scoring method. The strokes taken on each hole are added together. The lowest score wins. The lowest score can be either gross or net depending on whether handicap is deducted.

**FOUR BALL, BEST BALL**   As above, except that each team of two players submits only the best score on each hole. Two advantages: a bad player doesn't drag down the team score, and speed. A player's ball can be picked up without the automatic loss of the hole.

**FOURSOME: BEST BALL**   All four players play together. The team records only the best score. This game encourages risk taking and aggressive play.

**PINEHURST FOURSOMES**   All four players drive. Each team selects the best drive, and the other member of the team then takes the next shot. Handicap by adding together the two players' individual handicaps, halving, and deducting from the gross score at the end of the round.

**THROW OUT WORST HOLES**   Decide before the game how many holes may be discarded — usually it is three. Add together the strokes taken on these holes and deduct from the total.

**MATCH PLAY**   The winner is the player who wins more *holes* than his opponent (although it is quite possible that he will have taken more *strokes*). Holes are either won, drawn or lost. Clearly it is not necessary to play a full nine or eighteen holes before a winner emerges.

**FOUR BALL MATCH PLAY**   Use the best score on each team to determine the winner of the hole. Handicap by deducting the lowest handicap of all four players from the other three players.

**MATCH PLAY VERSUS PAR**   Add the number of times that the player beats par and deduct those that are lost to par. The player with the most positive (or least negative) score wins.

*Liberty.* September 17, 1932.
Baldy McCowen. Wood River Gallery.

# GOLF GAMES

**BISQUE PAR COMPETITION** Players get to deduct their handicap at will rather than as dictated on the scorecard. This enables better scores against par on difficult holes.

**POINT COMPETITION** The score at the end of each hole is rated by points, namely eight points for an eagle (two under par), six points for a birdie (one under par), four points for par and two points for bogey (one over par). All the above scores are net. Clearly, a disastrous hole will not have the same effect as in stroke play. It is also fast. If a player is not going to bogey, then the ball can be picked up.

**STABLEFORD** This is one of the basic — and oldest — forms of golf scoring. The scoring is four points for an eagle, three points for a birdie, two points for a par and one point for a bogey. Points are taken on net scores.

**CLOSEST TO PIN/LONGEST DRIVE** These two are very often used to add a little interest in tournaments. There needs to be a marker on which the name of the winning contestant (at any one point) can be written, and which will be placed on the spot where that ball has landed.

**GREENIE** The closest ball to the pin wins a point (or side bet). This is usually played on par-three holes.

**ONE/TWO/THREE-CLUB COMPETITION** This very challenging form of competition limits the golfer to playing the entire course with one, two or three clubs.

**CALLAWAY** Under the Callaway System, a player's handicap is determined after each round by deducting the worst individual scores a player makes during the first sixteen holes from the total eighteen holes. The table on page 111 shows the number of worst holes that may be deducted, as well as the adjustment. For instance, if the gross score for the eighteen holes is 96, the player turns to the table and opposite that score finds that he may deduct the total for his three worst holes scored on holes 1 through 16 inclusive. Thus, if he has one 9, one 8 and a 7, his handicap totals 24. From this total, a further plus or minus adjustment is made accordingly. (See adjustment at bottom of the table.)

# GOLF GAMES

| SCORE | | | | | DEDUCT | | | | |
|---|---|---|---|---|---|---|---|---|---|
| — | — | 70 | 71 | 72 | Scratch—No adjustment | | | | |
| 73 | 74 | 75 | — | — | ½ | worst hole plus adjustment | | | |
| 76 | 77 | 78 | 79 | 80 | 1 | " | " | " | " |
| 81 | 82 | 83 | 84 | 85 | 1½ | " | " | " | " |
| 86 | 87 | 88 | 89 | 90 | 2 | " | " | " | " |
| 91 | 92 | 93 | 94 | 95 | 2½ | " | " | " | " |
| 96 | 97 | 98 | 99 | 100 | 3 | " | " | " | " |
| 101 | 102 | 103 | 104 | 105 | 3½ | " | " | " | " |
| 106 | 107 | 108 | 109 | 110 | 4 | " | " | " | " |
| 111 | 112 | 113 | 114 | 115 | 4½ | " | " | " | " |
| 116 | 117 | 118 | 119 | 120 | 5 | " | " | " | " |
| 121 | 122 | 123 | 124 | 125 | 5½ | " | " | " | " |
| 126 | 127 | 128 | 129 | 130 | 6 | " | " | " | " |
| 131 | 132 | 133 | 134 | 135 | 6½ | " | " | " | " |
| 136 | 137 | 138 | 139 | 140 | 7 | " | " | " | " |

## ADJUSTMENT

| −2 | −1 | 0 | +1 | +2 | Add or adjust to handicap |
|---|---|---|---|---|---|

**Notes: 1.** No hole must be scored at more than twice its par.   **2.** Half strokes count as whole.   **3.** Holes 17 and 18 are never deducted.   **4.** Maximum handicap is 50.   **5.** In case of ties, lowest handicap takes preference.

Golfer.
Collection of Sarah Fabian Baddiel, London.

Designed by Martine Bruel
Photo Research by Picture Research Consultants
Composition in Playboy by the Composing Room of New England
Futura, Futura Book, and Bold by Hamilton Phototype
Color separations, printing, and binding by Tien Wah Press Ltd.